Fairy Affirmations

Positive Affirmations

Dedicated to:
7 G-Babies

Published by

INK Bubbles PUBLISHING

Port Elgin, Ontario,

Canada

2021

ISBN 978-1-7770829-4-9

FAIRY

AFFIRMATIONS

Positive Affirmations

CREATED BY JEWEL STAR

I am...
a good friend

I am... strong

I am...
helpful

I am... smart

I am... amazing

I am... kind

I am...
loved

I am... fun

I am... happy

I am...
awesome

I am... important

I am...
proud of myself

I am... special

I am... creative

I am... patient

I am... brave

I am... enough

I
love
me

Thank you for purchasing this book.

Follow Me on Instagram @Jewel Star Writer

Look for my other Children's Picture Books,

YA Books, Planners, Journals, Cookbooks,

Coloring Books, and other

genres.

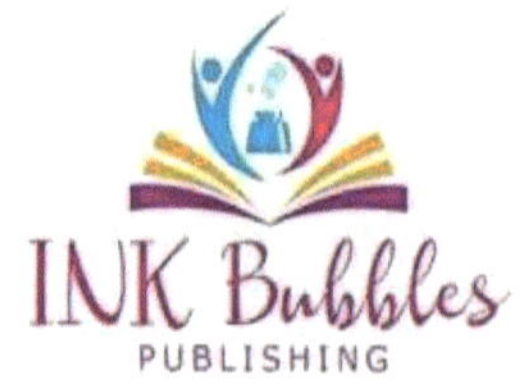

Published by INK Bubbles Publishing

2021

www.ingramcontent.com/pod-product-compliance
Lightning Source LLC
Chambersburg PA
CBHW042143030726
47599CB00002B/601